# DEMENTIA POEMS

Iris Therese Smith Reid wrote these poems along the way while looking after a husband who suffers from dementia and sickness. They were inspired by some of the things he has done and said while Iris has been his carer (for the last seven years now), his wife and his lifeline.

Since her husband was diagnosed with dementia Iris has kept a journal recording the many ways this tragic disorder has affected their daily life together.

The process of writing is one of the things that have helped her through this difficult time.

"Writing this and the poems," she says, "helps me recharge my batteries for what lies ahead."

# DEMENTIA POEMS

## Iris Therese Smith Reid

*Iris Therese Smith Reid*

ARTHUR H. STOCKWELL LTD
Torrs Park, Ilfracombe, Devon, EX34 8BA
*Established 1898*
*www.ahstockwell.co.uk*

*British Library Cataloguing-in-Publication Data.*
*A catalogue record for this book is available*
*from the British Library.*

ISBN 978-0-7223-4667-9
*Printed in Great Britain by*
*Arthur H. Stockwell Ltd*
*Torrs Park   Ilfracombe*
*Devon  EX34 8BA*

# CONTENTS

# DEMENTIA

I'll stay right beside you
For I know you have gone –
Let's hope not for ever,
Let's hope not for long.

My heart it starts hurting –
I'm feeling your pain.
This dementia it takes you
Again and again.

It's taken your memory,
It's taken your name.
You sit there just staring;
You look so downcast –
Your wife and your family
Are all in the past.

Your mind has all gone
On a different adventure
To a terrible sickness –
A thing called dementia.

I'll stay right beside you
For I know you have gone –
Let's hope not for ever,
Let's hope not for long.

# GONE

Where are my family?
I know they were here.
Why do they leave me?
Do none of them care?

I wake half the night
For I cannot sleep;
Thoughts of my family
Run far too deep.

I stumble along,
My mind full of fear,
My face full of agony,
My eyes full of tears.

One day they are here,
Next day there's none.
I saw them just yesterday,
But now they are gone.

Where are my family?
I know they were here.
Why do they leave me?
Do none of them care?

# LOST

You pecked at him meekly,
Just bits at a time.
You dug down there deeply
Right into his mind.

He was so happy
Till you came along;
Now most of his memory
Has nearly all gone.

You started off slowly
So no one would know,
But then you got daring
And stepped up your game.
You took without caring
And left him in pain.

It's not a pain
That you can cure –
Take a tablet
And it's no more.
It's a pain of not knowing
Who you are or where you're going.

You pecked at him meekly,
Just bits at a time.
You dug down there deeply
Right into his mind.

# ALONE

It's so very frightening
If you're on your own –
A feeling of knowing
That you're all alone.

But help is at hand
If only you knew –
There are plenty of people
Who want to help you.

There are millions just like him
That you have gone to,
But you carried on taking
Till everyone knew
Just what you were doing
And what they went through.

So they all joined together
Because they were sure –
If they carry on trying
They will find a cure.

It's so very frightening
If you're on your own –
A feeling of knowing
That you're all alone.

# SEARCHING

For him there's no rest,
For him no respite.
He walks around staring,
His face full of fright.

Searching for loved ones,
Searching for friends.
I cry when I see him,
I know he's in pain,
Wandering around pleading,
Searching in vain.

His face is so drained,
His face is so white –
He carries on searching
Well into the night,
But he never finds them,
They have all gone AWOL,
So he carries on searching,
A lost, lonely soul.

For him there's no rest,
For him no respite.
He walks around staring,
His face full of fright.

# STOLEN MINDS

So you damaged his mind,
So he sits there not knowing
Just who he is
Or where he is going.

You carry on taking –
You won't let him rest.
His mind is in turmoil –
You want what is left.

So now he's so sad,
He walks all alone,
And all that is left
Is his wife and his home.

So now he's a zombie.
You played with his mind,
You took without feeling –
You're cruel and unkind.

So now you have won,
You have taken your quarter,
You have gone to the mind
Of other sons and daughters.

So you damaged his mind,
So he sits there not knowing
Just who he is
Or where he is going.

# GOOD DAY

Today is a good day:
He is laughing out loud,
He knows all our names,
Is high on a cloud.

Sits answering quiz shows
And getting them right –
Had such a good day
And slept through the night.

Had a good conversation
With family and friends,
Dressed himself neatly
With no help of mine.

Helped in the garden,
Made himself tea,
Never stopped talking
And winking at me.

He was so happy,
So joyful, so gay,
And very much with us –
Another good day.

Today is a good day:
He is laughing out loud,
He knows all our names,
Is high on a cloud.

# BAD DAY

Some days are good days,
Some days are bad –
Don't know what he's thinking,
His face looks so sad.

He walks around crazily
Stumbling along.
Today he's not with us,
Today he has gone.

He looks so unhappy –
He's living in fear.
The sickness is with him –
There's no one else there.

Family go to him,
But what can they say?
They cannot help him –
It's another bad day.

Some days are good days,
Some days are bad –
Don't know what he's thinking,
His face looks so sad.

# LOST MEMORY, LOST MIND

Please can you help me?
Can you be so kind?
I think I've lost my memory,
I think I've lost my mind.

It wasn't so long ago
I remembered everything,
But now I have lost them –
I just don't know a thing.

I desperately need to find them.
I'm shouting way out loud.
Help me find my memory,
Help me find my mind.

I cannot think straight,
I don't know what to do –
My thoughts, my memories
Just will not come through.

Please can you help me?
Can you be so kind?
I think I've lost my memory,
I think I've lost my mind.

# LOST MY WAY

Please can you help me?
For I have lost my way.
Please can you help me?
I beg you, please, to stay.

Please can you help me?
For I have lost my home.
It was here not so long ago,
Of this I'm very sure,
But now I cannot find it –
It's standing here no more.

Please can you help me?
I've been looking all today,
Trying hard to find it,
But I have lost my way.

Please can you help me?
Don't leave me on my own.
Please can you help me?
I'm wanting to go home.

Please can you help me?
For I have lost my way.
Please can you help me?
I beg you, please, to stay.

# ON HIS HOLIDAY

"Are you enjoying it?"
He will say to me,
For he is on his holidays,
Which is not the same for me.

Going on a fishing boat,
Paddling in the bay,
Picking shells up off the beach,
Swimming in the sea.

I'm sitting right beside him
When he will say to me,
"When will we be going home?
I'm ready for my tea."

I tell him, "Yes, I'm loving it."
I don't want to be unkind,
For how can I be telling him
That it's all in his mind.

"Are you enjoying it?"
He will say to me,
For he is on his holidays,
Which is not the same for me.

# BACK IN TIME

It's been one month and a day
Since you wandered off,
Since you went away.

Going back to your army days,
Wandering back in time,
Twenty-five years of service,
Standing straight in line.

Building bridges,
Firing guns,
Christmas Island,
Atomic bombs.

Ireland and the IRA,
Trekking through the jungle,
Germany and Thailand,
Korea and Hong Kong.

How much longer
Will you roam?
When will you
Be coming home?

It's been one month and a day
Since you wandered off,
Since you went away.

# LOST WIFE

We sat together silently
When suddenly he said to me,
Looking shaken, eyes in fright,
"Where is she? Where is my wife?

"Has she gone out and about?"
I said to him, "Just look and see."
Pointing at myself: "It's me."
He stared at me,
His face so white,
"You're not her –
You're not my wife.

"Where is she? Where has she gone?
Where is she? Will she be long?"
He told me that he had to go,
But where to he did not know.

I told him, "You are not to worry,"
And not to be in such a hurry.
I told him just to wait one night
And everything would be all right.

We sat together silently
When suddenly he said to me,
Looking shaken, eyes in fright,
"Where is she? Where is my wife?"

# CONFUSED

He looks out the window,
His face all amused –
"That's a pretty light outside" –
And I know that he's confused.

I try hard to tell him,
Trying to explain
It's just a reflection
Of our light that's inside.

Then he gets anxious –
I cannot talk him round.
"If you don't secure it
It will all fall down."

One again I tell him,
Trying to explain
It's just a reflection,
But I'm trying in vain.

He looks out the window,
His face all amused –
"That's a pretty light outside" –
And I know that he's confused.

# LOST CHILDREN

"Where are my children?
Where can they be?
Where are my children?
Bring them to me."

"They're all grown-up
With children of their own.
They don't live with us –
We live all alone."

"Why did you not tell me?
Then I would have known
That I have children
Who have children of their own."

"I've told you so many times,
But I know you won't agree –
You never remember
Our children or me."

"Where are my children?
Where can they be?
Where are my children?
Bring them to me."

# AGITATED

He sits there all agitated,
Rattling his cane,
Displaying it left and right
Again and again.

Pacing up and down
With nothing to do,
Cussing and cursing
At I don't know who.

Waving his cane around
Up in the air –
Thank goodness it's only me,
No one else there.

I manage to calm him
And I always win;
Until he gets over it
I won't let him win.

He sits there all agitated,
Rattling his cane,
Displaying it left and right
Again and again.

# UPSET

He won't get out of bed –
He just lies there crying.
I can see that he's well upset,
But he must keep on trying.

"I cannot move my legs,
They both feel like lead.
I won't do a thing today –
I'll stay here in bed."

"Look, most days I feel the same,
Like you – I don't give in.
You cannot let it beat you,
You cannot let it win.

"Come on, get out of bed.
Have a nice cup of tea.
Then I will take you out
To see your grand-bairns with me."

He won't get out of bed –
He just lies there crying.
I can see that he's well upset,
But he must keep on trying.

# ANNOYED

"Come, put your coat on."
He keeps on saying no.
I see he is well annoyed –
He doesn't want to go.

"Stop being childish –
Do what you are told.
Help me put your coat on –
I don't want you catching cold.

"We have to go for your INR.
I don't want you to be late.
The sooner that you help me,
The sooner we know your fate."

"I'm not doing what you tell me,
I'm not doing what you say.
Don't talk to me that way –
And no, I won't catch cold."

"Come, put your coat on."
He keeps on saying no.
I see he is well annoyed –
He doesn't want to go.

# HELPING HANDS

I had no one that I could see;
I had no one to talk to me.
I thought that I was on my own,
Plodding along all alone.

There is help out there if only you know
Who to see and where to go –
Plenty of people who really care,
Knowing they are very near.

Finding out if they could be
Of any help to you and me –
It's a relief to finally know
Who to see and where to go.

I was feeling low
Until I found you
To help me along,
To see me through.

I had no one that I could see;
I had no one to talk to me.
I thought that I was on my own,
Plodding along all alone.

# GOING LOOPY

I think I'm going loopy –
It makes me feel so sad.
I repeat myself so many times
I think I'm going mad.

Sometimes I feel so down,
Sometimes I feel so blue.
I don't remember anything,
I just don't have a clue.

I do remember one thing,
Then suddenly it's gone.
If only I could get it right,
But I always get it wrong.

I tell myself it's morning
When in fact it's late at night,
Then I say it's getting dark
When in fact it's getting light.

I think I'm going loopy –
It makes me feel so sad.
I repeat myself so many times
I think I'm going mad.

# ON MY OWN

Since you've been gone,
For quite a while,
I get nothing from you,
Not even a smile.

You stumble along
Chanting a name –
You're so full of heartache,
You're so full of pain.

Where do you go to
When you wander away?
I know it's not your fault,
But I wish you would stay.

I do not like it
When I'm on my own;
I know you are with me,
But I'm still all alone.

Since you've been gone,
For quite a while,
I get nothing from you,
Not even a smile.

# CARE FOR YOU

Day and night I care for you,
I give you all my time,
But me the things I need to do
No one to care for mine.

I help you dress and shave,
I help you rest and bathe –
All the things I say and do
All because I care for you.

I take you for a drive,
I help you feel alive –
There is nothing I would not do
All because I care for you.

I am your nurse, your wife;
I am your friend for life.
Everything you need I do
All because I care for you.

We always go out and about,
We travel all the time –
There is nothing you need to do,
All because I care for you.

Day and night I care for you,
I give you all my time,
But me the things I need to do
No one to care for mine.

# NOT LISTENING

I said, "Watch your step
Or you will fall down."
Now you're flat on your face
And lying on the ground.

I said to be careful,
But you did not agree,
So what can I tell you?
For you cannot see.
So I've nothing to say –
You don't listen to me.

At least you're not hurt,
But too heavy by far
For I cannot get you
Back into the car.

But help is at hand
So there's nothing to fear –
Now you're back on your feet
Without even a care.

So now we can go
And be back on our way.
You don't listen to me,
So I've nothing to say.

# REPEATING YOURSELF

"Where is my pension book?"
You've asked me this before.
I've told you so many times;
I'm telling you no more.

I'm fed up of telling you,
Always asking me the same;
You're always repeating it
Over and over again.

You're doing my head in,
I don't know what to say.
You're always saying it to me –
I wish you'd go away.

I feel like a parrot,
Always answering to you,
But still you keep asking me
Till I don't know what to do.

"Where is my pension book?"
You've asked me this before.
I've told you so many times;
I'm telling you no more.

# CURED ME

"My toes and feet are hurting –
I'm lying here in pain."
"Here then, take this tablet –
It will cure you once again."

"How are your feet today?
The pain, has it all gone?"
"Yes, it has – you cured me.
It did not last for long."

"I've got an upset tummy –
It's hurting me again."
"Take a dose of this, then –
It will stop the pain."

"How is your tummy now?
The upset, has it gone?"
"Yes, it has – you cured me.
It did not last for long."

"My toes and feet are hurting –
I'm lying here in pain."
"Here then, take this tablet –
It will cure you once again."

# BRAINWASHED

I feel I'm being brainwashed –
The things you do and say.
You tell me that it's August
When in fact it's only May.

You even make me doubt myself
In everything I do.
I stop and have to check myself
And hope I've got it right.
You tell me it is morning
When in fact it's late at night.

I feel I'm being brainwashed
In everything I do.
I wonder if it could be me
And I don't know what to do.
Then I listen to what you say
And I know then that it's you.

I feel I'm being brainwashed –
The things you do and say.
You tell me that it's August
When in fact it's only May.

# HELPING OUT

I know you think you're doing great,
But you're not helping me
For everything you mend you break –
I wish you'd leave them be.

I've been watching what you do
And I wish that you would stop.
I don't want to upset you,
But I see you've lost the plot.

Everything that you have touched
You've ended up destroying.
I know you're only trying to help,
But to me it's so annoying.

I know you think you're helping,
But you're just upsetting me.
There was nothing wrong with them before,
So please don't mend them any more.

I know you think you're doing great,
But you're not helping me
For everything you mend you break –
I wish you'd leave them be.

# LOST GLASSES

"I've gone and lost my glasses,"
He will say to me.
"I've been looking everywhere –
Now I cannot see.

"I cannot read my paper,
I cannot read my book.
Will you help me find them?
Will you help me look?"

"You have to find them on your own –
I'm too busy here by far.
Have you checked your pockets?
Have you checked the car?"

"I wish you'd told me that before,
Then I would have known
That I would have to search for them
All on my very own."

"I've gone and lost my glasses,"
He will say to me.
"I've been looking everywhere –
Now I cannot see."

# LOST WALKING STICK

"I have lost my walking stick –
I don't know what to do.
If I cannot find it
I will have to lean on you."

"You are always losing things –
I hope you feel obliged.
If and when you find it,
Keep it by your side."

"Now I cannot walk far.
Now what can I do?"
"Don't go giving me that nonsense
For I know that you have two."

"I really need to find it –
I lose my balance all the time.
What's that lying on the ground?
Oh yes, that looks like mine."

"I have lost my walking stick –
I don't know what to do.
If I cannot find it
I will have to lean on you."

# NOT SLEEPING

For me it would be quite all right
If you would let me sleep,
For I need to close my eyes
And drift off into the deep.

If only you would keep awake.
You're sleeping all day long,
Then you stay awake all night –
You have got it all so wrong.

If only you would get it right
And I could have my way
Then I could sleep all night
And I could work all day.

I could give him a sleeping pill,
Then he would sleep all night.
But no, I don't believe in that
And it would not make it right.

For me it would be quite all right
If you would let me sleep,
For I need to close my eyes
And drift off into the deep.

# LOST CAT

Once we had a lovely cat –
Misty was her name.
One day I had to let her go –
For me it was a shame.

She followed him most everywhere,
Was with him all the while.
When he stopped walking so did she;
She always seemed to smile.

Some days I'd watch her stalking birds
And suddenly she would pounce.
I'm glad to say they got away
And she would look at me as if to say,
"Oh well, maybe another day."

He never looked before he sat –
He always dropped straight down,
And it was always on the cat.
It was him who let her down.

When I had to let her go
I cried most of the time,
For I loved her as much as he,
For she was also mine.

# FORGETTING THINGS

As soon as I remember things
I forget them once again,
And though I keep on trying
I know it's all in vain.

I leave my coat and hat –
I do it all the time –
And even when I do my best
I forget that they are mine.

I forget to shave when I am told,
I forget my scarf then I catch cold,
I forget my glasses and my tie,
I forget my stick and don't know why,
And though I'm trying all the time
I forget and leave them all behind.

As soon as I remember things
I forget them once again,
And though I keep on trying
I know it's all in vain.

# ACHES AND PAINS

"My arms and legs are aching –
I move them all the time.
It will be my circulation –
I'm sure it will be fine.

"I have a pain in my right eye –
It's really hurting me.
Now it's all gone bloodshot;
Now I cannot see."

"I know what you have to do
So that you can see:
You have to go to hospital.
They will laser it for you."

"My chest is also paining –
It pains me day and night."
"You have to see the doctor –
He will make it right."

"Now I have a headache
And don't know what to do.
Now I have a headache
And that headache is you."

# WANDERING OFF

"I'm going off to catch a bus,"
He tells me with a smile.
"Hang on a mo – what is your rush?
Stop and talk a while.

"Where is it that you want to go?
Where is it that you're going?"
"I cannot say – I do not know.
I don't know what I'm doing."

"You must never wander on your own
Not knowing where you're going
You might not find your way back home
And no one would be knowing."

"I'm going off to catch a bus,"
He tells me with a smile.
"Hang on a mo – what is your rush?
Stop and talk a while."

# OUT AND ABOUT

I'll push you through the park today
We're going for fresh air,
We can feed the ducks along the way.
The weather will be fair.

We can meet with friends and sit and talk
And watch the ducks at play
Then you can have a little walk
Before we go on our way.

It's so relaxing in the park,
But we will not be stopping.
We must be home before it's dark –
I have to do my shopping.

We did enjoy our time today,
But now we have to go.
We will be back another day,
But when I do not know.

I'll push you through the park today
We're going for fresh air,
We can feed the ducks along the way.
The weather will be fair.

# GOING TO WORK

"I've got to go to work today –
I'd better not be late."
"You haven't worked for twenty years –
I think you'd better wait.

"Your work it is all finished now;
It isn't there no more.
Everything is all closed down –
I've told you this before."

"You don't ever need to work no more
You're well past eighty-four
Don't keep saying you have to go –
Come back and close the door."

"I've got to go to work today –
I'd better not be late."
"You haven't worked for twenty years –
I think you'd better wait."

# SMILE

Why is it that you look so sad?
Your place right here is not that bad.
Come on, give me a little smile.
Come on, be happy for a while.

To put that smile back on your face
I know just what to do.
I'll take you to a nicer place –
I'll take you to the zoo.

Lots of pets and wildlife there,
Lots of things to see.
Come on, show me that you care –
Give up a smile for me.

I know you had a lovely time –
I noticed that big smile.
I know that it turned out fine,
I know it was worthwhile.

Why is it that you look so sad?
Your place right here is not that bad.
Come on, give me a little smile.
Come on, be happy for a while.

# UNWELL

"You did not eat at all today –
You're looking quite unwell.
You're looking rather 'peakish' –
I know, for I can tell."

"Oh, do stop all your fussing!
Will you leave me be!
I did have something today –
I had a drink of tea."

"Look, I am your carer –
I know what to do.
I have to know that you're all right –
I must take care of you.

"I'll take you to the doctor –
It will not take us long.
He will just examine you;
He will know what's wrong.

"You did not eat at all today –
You're looking quite unwell.
You're looking rather 'peakish' –
I know, for I can tell."

# LOST HUSBAND

Where is he,
The man that used to be?
That's not him standing there.
That's not the man I married,
The man that used to care.

He used to be so loving,
Was with me all the time;
Now there's just a shell of him
Who never will be mine.

I've lost him now forever.
If only I had known.
All I know is that's not him –
I'm left here on my own.

I always lived in hope,
Not knowing if I'd cope,
But now I know it's not to be –
He never will return to me.

Where is he,
The man that used to be?
That's not him standing there.
That's not the man I married,
The man that used to care.

# ANGRY

Why do you get so angry?
You only have to say.
No need to shout at me like that
Because you want your way.

I only do what's best for you,
I only wish you'd see.
It's no good feeling sorry –
You'd do the same for me.

It's no good trying it alone –
There's nothing you can do.
You cannot do it on your own –
You know that it takes two.

I know you have a broken foot
And you cannot put on your shoes,
So let me put them on for you –
It's the least that I can do.

Why do you get so angry?
You only have to say.
No need to shout at me like that
Because you want your way.

# BLAMING ME

He stands there shouting frantically
While he ties himself in knots,
For he cannot dress himself
And he's blaming it on me.

Come on, stop your shouting.
Come on, let it be.
You have to swallow all your pride
And accept some help from me.

It's not my fault you're struggling –
It's no good blaming me.
I know you've got a useless arm –
Let me help you and you'll see.

I know you won't admit it,
I know you have your pride.
You know you can depend on me,
And you can say you always tried.

He stands there shouting frantically
While he ties himself in knots,
For he cannot dress himself
And he's blaming it on me.

# STAY WITH ME

Did I hear you right?
Did you call my name?
Yes, you're back with me again.
How long for? I'll wait and see
How long that you'll stay with me.

I must admit I did not know
If you would stay or go.
I only know I missed you so –
I waited patiently.
I wish you never had to go
And you would stay with me.

Now I know that it's not so
And that it has to be.
At least today you're here with me.
There's no saying for how long –
I will have to wait and see
For I know you'll soon be gone.

Did I hear you right?
Did you call my name?
Yes, you're back with me again.
How long for? I'll wait and see
How long you're going to stay with me.

# IN YOUR MIND

"What is it that you're looking for?
You've been looking quite some time.
Because they're only in your mind,
They're things that you won't find.

"Now it's started raining –
Now you're getting wet.
Come back inside before you catch a cold."
"But I haven't found it yet.

"I don't know what I'm looking for –
It's something I must find,
Something that I won't forget,
Something that's on my mind."

"What is it that you're looking for?
You've been looking quite some time.
Because they're only in your mind,
They're things that you won't find."

# DON'T GO

Don't leave again – please don't go.
I wish that you could stay.
I know that it's not your fault
That you have to go away.

I know I always live in fear,
I know I live in hope,
Not knowing if you're staying here,
Not knowing if I'll cope.

When will you be coming home?
My life is standing still.
When will you be coming back?
That's if you ever will.

I know that you would stay here –
You wouldn't leave me on my own.
I know you really care –
You wouldn't leave me all alone.

Don't leave again – please don't go.
I wish that you could stay.
I know that it's not your fault
That you have to go away.

# CHRISTMAS DAY

Will you stop your moaning!
Everything will turn out fine.
Today is such a special day
Because it's Christmas time.

I'll push you in your wheelchair –
We're off to see the lights.
They really are fantastic
If you watch them late at night.

Look at that big Christmas tree
Standing in the square.
I've never seen so many baubles –
They're hanging everywhere.

Look at all them penguins
Dancing up and down
And that lit-up snowman
Moving along the ground.

They all look like they're moving
Because they're flashing off and on.
I must admit I'm loving it –
I'm having so much fun.

Will you stop your moaning!
Everything will turn out fine.
Today is such a special day
Because it's Christmas time.

# COMING AND GOING

Suddenly he does not know
Where he is or where to go,
Wandering here, wandering there,
Does not know, does not care,
Blindly going nowhere.

Mostly thinking, 'Where am I?'
Spending time wondering why –
Mostly thinking, him not knowing,
Wandering around, coming and going.

Suddenly he will know who he is
And where to go.
He will know where he has been,
He will know what he has seen.

Suddenly he does not know
Where he is or where to go,
Wandering here, wandering there,
Does not know, does not care,
Blindly going nowhere.

# A BRAVE, A BROKEN SOLDIER

When I moan
About my knee
I look at you.
What do I see?
Everything that you go through –
A brave, a broken soldier.

The way you walk dragging your leg,
The way you get up out of bed,
The way you turn a lot of heads.
Everything that you go through –
A brave, a broken soldier.

The way you wander aimlessly,
The way you wander blindingly,
The way you walk so painfully.
Everything that you go through –
A brave, a broken soldier.

A weakened heart,
A broken foot,
A blinded eye.
When I look
What do I see?
Everything that you go through –
A brave, a broken soldier.

# I'M ALWAYS THERE

I know that you don't walk far.
You cannot get up and down.
I know that it's the way you are
And it's hard to get around.

Don't worry, you can lean on me.
You don't have to stay.
Lots of things I do, you'll see,
To help you on your way.

You know you can depend on me –
You won't be on your own.
You know I'll help you, wait and see –
You won't be left alone.

All the things I ever do –
You know I'm always there.
I'll always take good care of you;
I always will be here.

I know that you don't walk far.
You cannot get up and down.
I know that it's the way you are
And it's hard to get around.

# WHERE DO YOU GO TO?

Where is it that you go to?
You tell me you don't know.
I never know where you have been,
I never know what you have seen.

Why do you have to go away?
It always makes me worry.
Why is it that you never stay?
You leave in such a hurry.

I'm happy when you do return
Because I always care.
I'm happy that you've come back home,
Then I've no need to fear.

I wonder where you go to –
I only wish I knew.
I wish I could go with you –
It's the first thing I would do.

Where is it that you go to?
You tell me you don't know.
I never know where you have been,
I never know what you have seen.

# YOU DON'T RETAIN IT

I know you don't retain it –
You don't remember things for long.
You remember things for just one day
Then tomorrow they're all gone.

You don't know where you're going
When you go on your way.
I hate to see you on your own
And suffering that way.

Why do I keep on telling you?
I know it won't sink in.
I know I'm wasting all my time –
I know I'll never win.

I wish that I could stop it –
I know I'll always try.
To me it would be such a sin
If I just let dementia win.

You take up all my energy,
You take up all my time.
I don't want it any other way –
To me you're always mine.

I know you don't retain it –
You don't have a clue.
You don't know what you're doing
And there's nothing I can do.

# DON'T PUSH HIM DOWN

Will you stop that pushing!
Will you let him be!
Just because he cannot walk
As fast as you and me.

He's got a broken foot –
You could be the same –
It should make you stop and think
And make you feel ashamed.

Don't be in such a hurry,
Don't be so unkind.
Give a man that cannot walk
Five minutes of your time.

Will you stop that pushing!
Let him walk that little way,
Then to your friends you can say
You've done your best today.

He's not the same as you or me –
He cannot get up and go.
Your mother would not like you
If she should ever know.

Just because you cannot wait
Stop pushing him around.
Don't push him out the way,
Don't push him to the ground.

# I NEVER GET A READ

After you have read the paper it's no good to me –
The way you throw it all around,
Then scatter it upon the ground.
I never get a read.

It never stays all in one piece
No matter what I say.
You screw it up, tear it in bits,
Then throw it all away.

It won't go back together –
It's too torn up by far.
I ask you, "Let me read it first."
But no, you don't know how.

Why do you keep on doing that
After it's been read?
Is it something that I did
Or something that I said?

You tell me that you're sorry –
You don't know what you do.
I blame it on your sickness,
There's no way I blame you.

# LEARNING ALONG THE WAY

I know he's got dementia –
Tell me something new.
I've coped with it for seven years,
Not knowing what to do.

Going through the good times,
Going through the bad,
Sometimes having happy days,
Sometimes having sad.

There's nothing you can tell me –
I learn it as I go.
There's nothing I don't see,
There's nothing I don't know.

He keeps me up all night,
He keeps me up all day.
I don't always get it right,
But I learn along the way.

I know he's got dementia –
Tell me something new.
I've coped with it for seven years,
Not knowing what to do.

# CHEEKY BUGGER

"I'm going to tell my nurse on you
While you sit on your bum –
All the work you make me do
While you sit having fun."

"Oh, you cheeky bugger!
You've only taken out one cup.
Next time that you take it out
You can wash it up."

"My nurse told me I had to rest
For I'm a poorly man.
But no, I do my very best,
Working all I can."

"Oh, you cheeky bugger!
You've only taken out one cup.
Next time that you take it out
You can wash it up."

"I'm in and out all day,
Taking pots out on the way.
My nurse would be so mad at you
If she found out the work I do."

"Oh, you cheeky bugger!
You've only taken out one cup.
Next time that you take it out
You can wash it up."

# GOING FOR A WALK

"I'm going for my walk now."
"Well, don't be going far.
Sometimes you lose your way
And don't know where you are."

"I'm only walking to the gate –
You can watch and see,
The way you always do
When you're watching out for me."

"Don't go walking in the street –
Make sure you turn around.
You're unsteady on your feet –
I don't want you falling down.

"Make sure you put your coat on,
It's very cold out there."
"I will. I won't be gone for long –
I know how much you care."

"I'm going for my walk now."
"Well, don't be going far.
Sometimes you lose your way
And don't know where you are."

# CHEEKY MONKEY

"Are we going out today?
I'm sick of sitting in this chair –
You never take me anywhere.
There's an imprint of my bum in there."

"Oh, you cheeky monkey!
I take you everywhere.
You never sit for long,
Especially in your chair.

"I always take you out,
You're always having fun.
If you don't be careful
I'll leave an imprint on your bum."

"You always keep me in.
We don't go out for long.
We don't go very far.
You're the one who's always wrong."

"Oh, you cheeky monkey!
I've a mind to box your ears.
I would if I could get away with it,
But it would only end in tears."

# TALK TO ME

Tell me what is wrong with you –
You have not said one word.
I could make it go away
If only you would say.

I am not a mind reader.
I don't want to be unkind –
If only you would talk to me
I would know what's on your mind.

I only want to help you –
I don't know what is wrong.
I don't know what to do –
I only want it gone.

If you don't confide in me
It will never go.
If you do not let me see
Then I will never know.

Tell me what is wrong with you –
You have not said one word.
I could make it go away
If only you would say.

# FULL OF WIND

You're in and out this house
Like you've never done before,
Running like the clappers
In and out the door.

I know there's something wrong,
By that look upon your face.
You're looking very shifty,
Running in and out all day.
I know you're up to something –
Whatever it is just say.

I think I'll stop and listen –
I don't trust you any more
The way you are behaving,
Running in and out the door.

I'll just have to follow you,
Keeping by your side.
I'll find out what you're up to
And what you have to hide.

So now I've found out what it is:
I heard you blowing off outside.
Until you're rid of all that wind
You're not coming back inside.

# WHEN ARE WE GOING HOME?

Every day you say the same:
"When are we going home?"
I tell you we're already here.
You say I should have told you so
And then you would have known.

I don't know where you think you are –
You tell me you don't know.
You tell me that it is not far
And that we have to go.

You ask me if I know the way,
How long would we be gone?
I tell him we're already here –
It did not take us long.

He said, "I'm glad I've come back home.
I don't know where I've been.
I thought that I was all alone
And never would be seen."

Every day you say the same:
"When are we going home?"
I tell you we're already here.
You say I should have told you so
And then you would have known.

# WE TREASURE OUR MEMORIES

We don't know what's coming,
We don't know our fate.
We treasure our memories
Before it's too late.

We sit watching waves
Running over the sand,
We sit watching mountains
Reaching down to the land.

We sit watching daytime
Turn into night,
We sit watching ships
With all their bright lights.

We sit watching birds
Flying over the sea.
We treasure our memories –
They're ours, you and me.

Treasure your memories –
They might not last long,
Because when tomorrow comes
They all could be gone.

We don't know what's coming,
We don't know our fate.
We treasure our memories
Before it's too late.

# HAPPY AND SECURE

He sits there in his garden
Like so many times before,
For it is the only place
He feels happy and secure.

Watching pretty butterflies
Dancing in the breeze,
Watching all the little birds
Eating up the seeds.

Watching lots of busy bees
Flying everywhere,
Diving down upon the flowers
Throwing their scent into the air.

The sun goes in, it starts to rain,
It's falling all around.
He watches it run down the drain
And wetting all the ground.

The sun's back out, all is refreshed,
It dries up all the rain,
Then he feels so happy
And sits watching once again.

He sits there in his garden
Like so many times before,
For it is the only place
He feels happy and secure.

# GOING ROUND IN CIRCLES

Going on his daily walk
Then resting on his cane,
Going round in circles
Then repeating it again.

Walking round and round,
Singing as he goes,
Doesn't know he's just been there –
Does not even care.

Turned and went the other way,
Started walking up and down,
Stopped to have a little rest
Then carried on walking round and round.

Turning to the front,
Walking half the day,
Turning round again
And walking back the other way.

Going on his daily walk
Then resting on his cane,
Going round in circles
Then repeating it again.